First Facts®

Faceless, Spineless, and Brainless Ocean Animals

JELLYFISH

by Jody S. Rake

Consultant:
Dr. Deborah Donovan
Professor, Biology Department and Science Education Group
Western Washington University
Bellingham, Washington

CAPSTONE PRESS
a capstone imprint

First Facts are published by Capstone Press,
1710 Roe Crest Drive, North Mankato, Minnesota 56003
www.mycapstone.com

Library of Congress Cataloging-in-Publication Data
Names: Rake, Jody Sullivan, author.
Title: Jellyfish / by Jody S. Rake.
Description: North Mankato, Minnesota : Capstone Press, [2017] | Series:
   First facts. Faceless, spineless, and brainless ocean animals | Audience:
   Ages 7-9.? | Audience: K to grade 3.? | Includes bibliographical references and index.
Identifiers: LCCN 2015051429 | ISBN 9781515721499 (eBook PDF) | ISBN 9781515721413
(hardcover) | ISBN 9781515721451 (pbk.)
Subjects: LCSH: Jellyfishes—Juvenile literature.
Classification: LCC QL377.S4 R354 2017 | DDC 593.5/3—dc23
LC record available at http://lccn.loc.gov/2015051429

Editorial Credits
Abby Colich, editor; Bobbie Nuytten, designer; Kelly Garvin, media researcher; Steve Walker,
production specialist

Photo Credits
Minden Pictures/Richard Herrmann, 7; Nature Picture Library/Aflo, 20; Newscom/Educational
Images Ltd./Custom Medical Stock Photo "CMSP Biology", 15; SeaPics/David Wrobel, 17;
Shutterstock: Edwin Verin, 5, 11, Glenn Young, 21, Pavel Vakhrushev, cover, 1, Rich Carey, 19,
stephan kerkhofs, 9, Zacarias Pereira da Mata, 13

Artistic Elements
Shutterstock: Artishok, Vikasuh

Printed and bound in China

PO007692RRDF16

Table of Contents

No Bones, No Problem

Do you know of any animals that don't have any bones? The sea is full of boneless creatures. They don't even have a backbone, or spine. Animals without spines are **invertebrates**. Jellyfish are invertebrates. They don't have a brain, eyes, or ears. Other body parts help them move and find food.

invertebrate—an animal without a backbone

Fact! A group of jellyfish is called a "bloom" or "smack."

Jellyfish Big and Small

There are more than 200 **species** of jellyfish. They live in every ocean. Some glide in warm, shallow water. Others slink through the dark, deep sea. Some jellyfish display dazzling colors. Others look like they're made of clear glass.

Jellyfish can be many sizes. Some are as small as 0.5 inch (1.3 centimeters) wide. Others are as big as 6 feet (1.8 meters) wide.

species—a group of creatures that are capable of reproducing with one another

Fact! The deepest jellyfish ever found was 8,530 feet (2,600 m) below the water's surface.

7

JellyFish Bells

Jellyfish have soft, round bodies called bells. Under the bell is a mouth. Food goes into the mouth. Waste and **reproductive cells** go out the mouth. The bell contains a stomach and other body parts. Hanging from the bell are many **tentacles**. Tentacles can be short or long. Some jellyfish have only a few tentacles. Others have hundreds.

reproductive cell—a male or female cell needed to make offspring
tentacle—a long, armlike body part some animals use to touch, grab, or smell

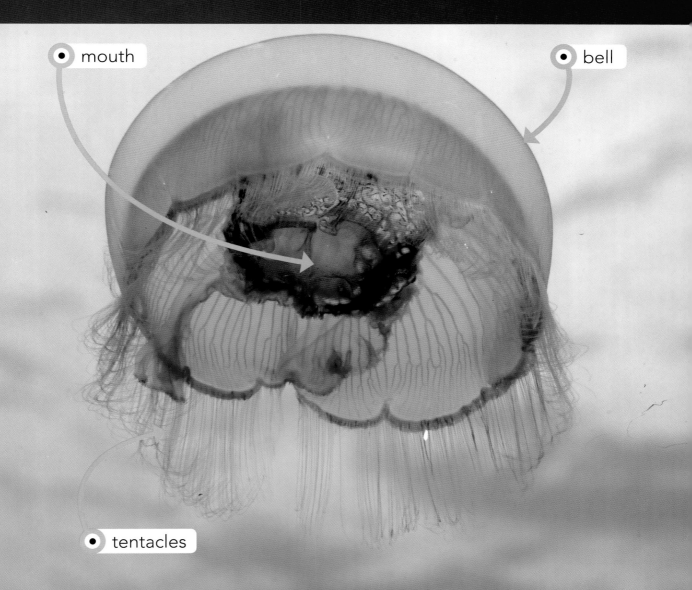

mouth

bell

tentacles

Jellyfish Jam

How do jellyfish move without fins or flippers? Sometimes they drift through the ocean. The water carries them. They can also move by squeezing their bells. They push water out, moving themselves forward.

Fact! Some jellyfish have oral arms in addition to tentacles. Oral arms work like tentacles to help the jellyfish catch food.

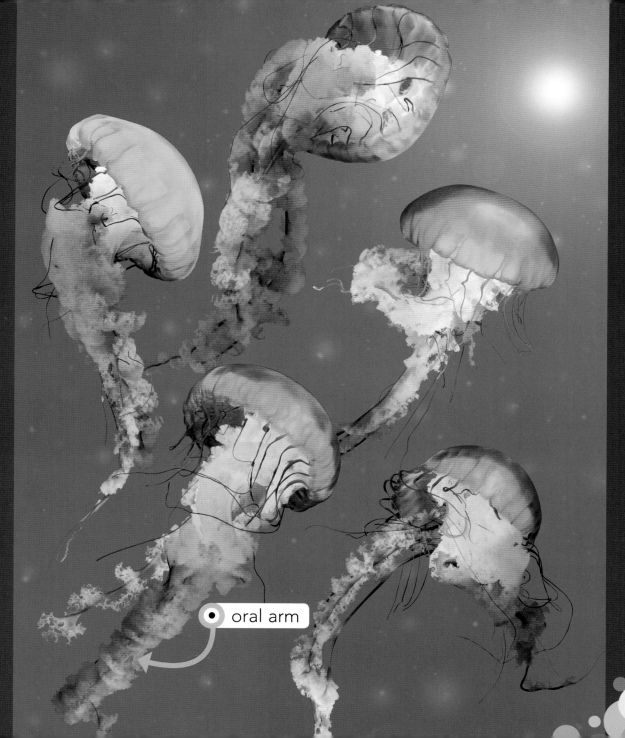

oral arm

No Brain Needed

Jellyfish don't have brains. Instead they have a **nerve net**. The nerve net surrounds the jellyfish's body. It helps the jellyfish move and find food. Some jellyfish have nerves that let them sense light.

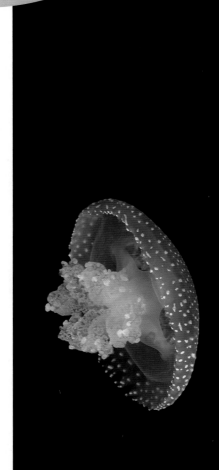

Fact! Some jellyfish have cells that create light, or **bioluminescence**. The light confuses **predators**. This lets the jellyfish escape.

nerve net—a system of thin strands in the body that carry messages
bioluminescence—the production of light by a living organism
predator—an animal that hunts another animal for food

It's a Sting Thing

Small jellyfish eat **plankton**. Larger ones feast on fish, shrimp, and other jellyfish. Tentacles catch a jellyfish's food. **Prey** brushes against the tentacles. Then the tentacles sting the prey. The helpless prey is slowly pulled into the jellyfish's mouth and swallowed whole.

plankton—tiny organisms that drift in the sea
prey—an animal hunted by another animal for food
venom—a poison an animal makes to kill its prey

How Tentacles Sting

Each tentacle is covered with tiny, stinging cells. Each cell holds a dart. The dart is connected to a tube. The tube carries **venom**. When prey touches the tentacles, the dart shoots venom into the victim.

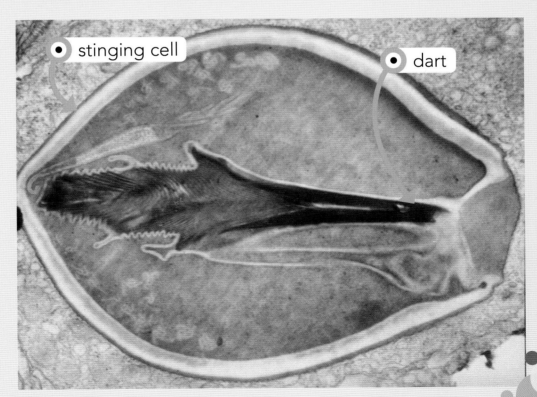

stinging cell

dart

Jellyfish Life Cycle

Female jellyfish release eggs into the sea. Males release sperm. The eggs and sperm meet. Then they grow into **larvae**. The larvae drift until they attach to an object. Then they grow into **polyps**. Polyps look like little flowers. The polyps grow layers. The layers bud off into young jellyfish.

Are Jellyfish at Risk?

Some jellyfish are food for humans. But they are not overfished. Jellyfish numbers may actually be on the rise. Why? Jellyfish easily **adapt**. They can survive changes in the ocean that other sea animals cannot.

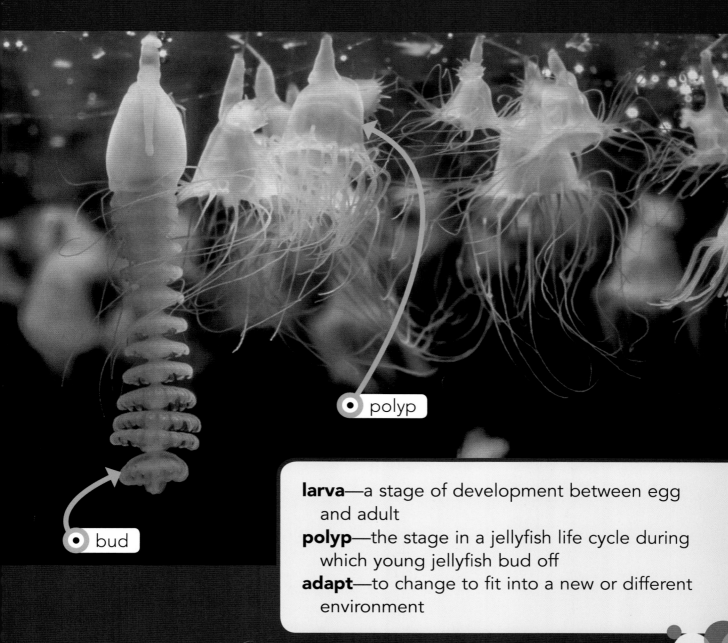

polyp

bud

larva—a stage of development between egg and adult
polyp—the stage in a jellyfish life cycle during which young jellyfish bud off
adapt—to change to fit into a new or different environment

Jellyfish Threats

Most predators avoid jellyfish. They don't want to tangle with the tentacles. But some animals eat jellyfish in spite of the sting. They are a favorite meal of sea turtles. Other predators include sunfish, mackerel, and dogfish sharks.

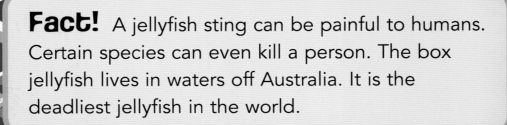

Fact! A jellyfish sting can be painful to humans. Certain species can even kill a person. The box jellyfish lives in waters off Australia. It is the deadliest jellyfish in the world.

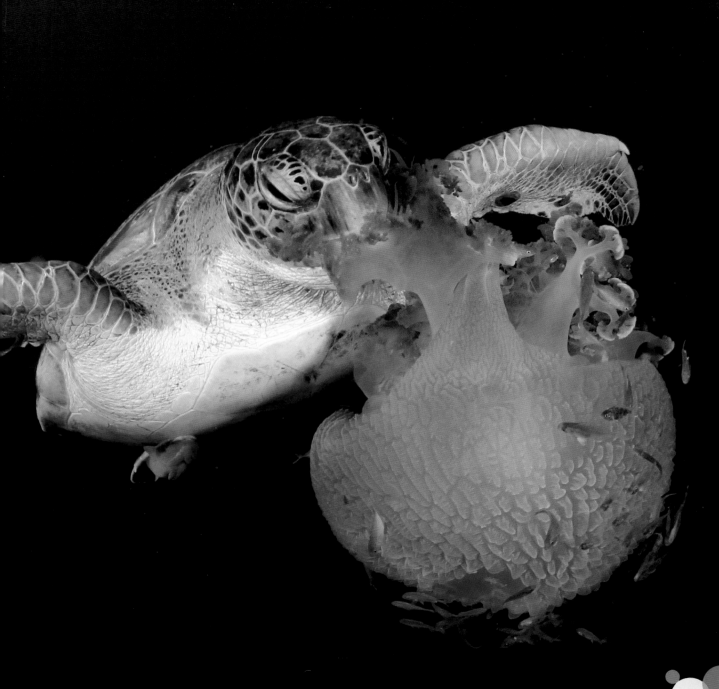

Amazing But True!

One jellyfish species has earned the nickname "immortal jellyfish." When threatened, an adult can return to the polyp stage. Then it will grow all over again. This behavior is a response to injury or lack of food.

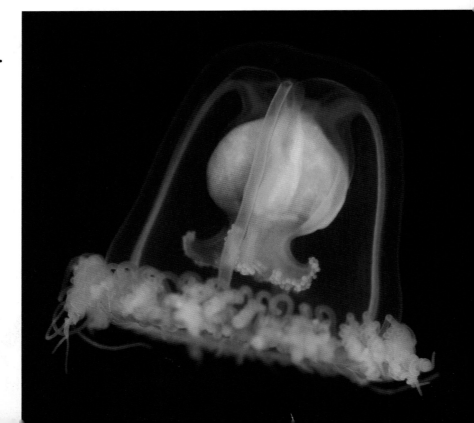

Jellyfish Facts

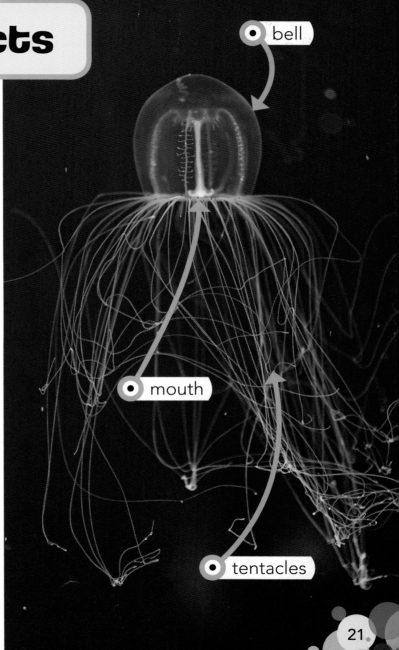

bell

mouth

tentacles

Where it lives: oceans worldwide

Habitat: found in all ocean habitats

Size: 0.5 inch (1.3 cm) to more than 6 feet (1.8 m) wide

Diet: plankton, krill, shrimp, small fish, other jellyfish

Predators: sea turtles, fish, sharks

Life span: a few months on average; can range from a few days to 2 or 3 years

Status: stable (not at risk of dying out)

Glossary

adapt (uh-DAPT)—to change to fit into a new or different environment

bioluminescence (BUY-oh-loo-muh-ne-senss)—the production of light by a living organism

invertebrate (in-VUR-tuh-bruht)—an animal without a backbone

larva (LAR-vuh)—a stage of development between egg and adult

nerve net (NURV NET)—a system of thin strands in the body that carry messages

plankton (PLANGK-tuhn)—tiny organisms that drift in the sea

polyp (PAH-lupp)—the stage in a jellyfish life cycle during which young jellyfish bud off

predator (PRED-uh-tur)—an animal that hunts another animal for food

prey (PRAY)—an animal hunted by another animal for food

reproductive cell (ree-pruh-DUCK-tiv SELL)—a male or female cell needed to make offspring

species (SPEE-sheez)—a group of creatures that are capable of reproducing with one another

tentacle (TEN-tuh-kuhl)—a long, armlike body part some animals use to touch, grab, or smell

venom (VEN-uhm)—a poison an animal makes to kill its prey

Read More

Gibbs, Maddie. *Jellyfish*. Powerkids Readers: Fun Fish. New York: PowerKids Press, 2014.

Marsico, Katie. *Jellyfish*. Nature's Children. New York: Children's Press, 2015.

Owen, Ruth. *Box Jellyfish*. Real Life Sea Monsters. New York: PowerKids Press, 2014.

Internet Sites

FactHound offers a safe, fun way to find Internet sites related to this book. All of the sites on FactHound have been researched by our staff.

Here's all you do:

Visit *www.facthound.com*

Type in this code: 9781515721413

 Check out projects, games and lots more at
www.capstonekids.com

Critical Thinking Using the Common Core

1. Name a jellyfish body part and describe how it helps them survive. (Key Idea and Details)

2. Reread the text on page 6 and study the photo on page 7. Then study another photo of a jellyfish in the book. Describe how they are different. Then describe what likenesses they have that make them both jellyfish. (Craft and Structure)

3. Reread page 10. What if jellyfish had bones? How might they move differently? (Integration of Knowledge and Ideas)

Index